PICTLAN]
THE CONVERSION TO CHRISTIANITY OF A PAGAN RACE

Dedication

To the staff and members of Gloucester Park Day Centre, Larne, and to Hilary Alexander, who works there.

PICTLAND:
THE CONVERSION TO
CHRISTIANITY OF A PAGAN RACE

Michael Sheane

ARTHUR H. STOCKWELL LTD
Torrs Park, Ilfracombe, Devon, EX34 8BA
Established 1898
www.ahstockwell.co.uk

ISBN 978-0-7223-5034-8
Printed in Great Britain by
Arthur H. Stockwell Ltd
Torrs Park   Ilfracombe
Devon EX34 8BA

By the same author:

Ulster & Its Future After the Troubles (1977)
Ulster & The German Solution (1978)
Ulster & The British Connection (1979)
Ulster & The Lords of the North (1980)
Ulster & The Middle Ages (1982)
Ulster & St Patrick (1984)
The Twilight Pagans (1990)
Enemy of England (1991)
The Great Siege (2002)
Ulster in the Age of Saint Comgall of Bangor (2004)
Ulster Blood (2005)
King William's Victory (2006)
Ulster Stock (2007)
Famine in the Land of Ulster (2008)
Pre-Christian Ulster (2009)
The Glens of Antrim (2010)
Ulster Women – A Short History (2010)
The Invasion of Ulster (2010)
Ulster in the Viking Age (2011)
Ulster in the Eighteenth Century (2011)
Ulster in the History of Ireland (2012)
Rathlin Island (2013)
Saint Patrick's Missionary Journeys in Ireland (2015)
The Story of Carrickfergus (2015)
Ireland's Holy Places (2016)
The Conqueror of the North (2017)
The Story of Holywell Hospital: A Country Asylum (2018)
Patrick: A Saint for All Seasons (2019)
The Picts: The Painted People (2019)

The middle years of the first millennium AD saw North Britain emerging from the collapse of the Roman Empire in the country – commonly known as the Dark Ages. The Picts fought each other while society reverted to cultural ignorance and a primitive way of life. In Europe the barbarians were starting to write their own histories. The Dark Ages may be defined as the period that elapsed from the withdrawal of the Roman legions to the coming of the Normans in the twelfth century. After the fall of Rome, Britain deteriorated into a number of petty kingdoms ruled by literate kings. The Christian clergy now compiled accounts of the Picts and their other neighbours. Modern historians use the term Early Historic Period instead of the Dark Ages.

In the north, two large and powerful groups guarded the Forth–Clyde line. The Picts responded to this by stiffening their resolve in regard to their own identity. Why this happened is not known, but the Picts could be seen as a loosely defined nation often called Pictavia, which means simply Pictland. When historians refer to the Picts in a political sense, what they are really speaking of is the upper strata of society – the kings and high-ranking clergy, and aristocratic war bands whose strength gave them the idea of absolute kingship.

But what is the meaning of the term 'kingship' in the context of sixth-century Pictland? To answer this question we have to look at the life of the Pictish upper classes from whom the kings were drawn, and also at Pictish life as a whole. The Picts, however, were not very different from other barbarian peoples beyond the frontiers of the Roman Empire. Despite their location in the northern parts of Britain they were not isolated from their neighbours nor impervious to external influences. By the beginning of the sixth century the Pictish nation was no longer a patchwork of tribes seen on Ptolemy's map, but a group of small provinces or subkingdoms whose identity more or less related in some way to the seven regions named in the legend of Cruithne. Continuity with the remote past was maintained by a recognition that the nations were divided into two parts. Irish and English writers of the seventh and eighth centuries classified Pictland as being divided into two regions – the northern and southern areas – separated by the Grampian Mountains, otherwise known as Mounth. The divide, whose roots lay deep in history, was geographical rather than human, and the Picts maintained a well-defined cultural unity in spite of it.

The Picts used symbols not common elsewhere, undoubtedly of very ancient origin, having been created in prehistory as a form of alphabet; they appear to have decorated jewellery or even tattoos, but their use changed after the Roman era. By AD 500 these symbols were beginning to appear as carvings on standing stones and were common over a great area, on Orkney, Skye and Shetland and in Perthshire. All these areas boasted high-status Picts. The meanings of the symbols are unknown, but the lure of solving the problem remains. Various theories have been proposed. Some theories point to the symbols as emblems of important families linked by marriage alliances; other theories see the symbols relating to nature or agriculture. But none of these beliefs appear to be likely.

One theory sees the symbols as representations of personal names; the symbols appear to have an origin in the late fifth or early sixth centuries. The symbols were created at a time when other symbols were appearing in other parts of Britain. The Pictish stones perhaps served as grave markers for Christians. The 'writing' on them may point to a dead parent. A similar alphabet of emblems to identify an individual or their families was used effectively in medieval times, and this could have its origins in Pictish heraldry. The Pictish symbols were perhaps a code or alphabet by which a person's name could be easily identified in a society where conventional writing was unknown.

Culturally, then, the Picts were defined as a group who possessed an artistic tradition that was unique in the British Isles. In this respect they were little different from other barbarian peoples in northern Europe. Barbarian society in the Dark Ages (the Early Historic Period) had long since abandoned egalitarian traits and was highly stratified in the way of wealth and status, with the bulk of the peasantry living off the land, ruled by a king and his aristocracy. Tacitus and other classical writers presented a stereotyped view of the Picts, who went around in ragged furs, but such phenomena may not have originated in Roman propaganda.

By the start of the sixth century the Pictish aristocracy was a wealthy upper class with expensive tastes and a luxurious lifestyle. Its members were a selective elite holding absolute power over the peasants, which comprised the majority of the population. Peasants were unlikely to be free farmers working in the fields, and were perhaps bound to the land of their lord, having few privileges and with minimal rights under the Pictish law. They almost certainly took an active role in warfare. In most parts of the British Isles, during the Dark Ages or the Early Historic Period, the peasants were excluded from military service. There was no mass mobilization of agricultural labourers armed with crude weapons – no local militia like the Anglo-Saxon fyrd of the tenth century. Like hunting and feasting, war was the exclusive pursuit of the landowning classes, and it provided a career for the ambitious young noblemen. War brought the prospect to the noblemen of wealth and fame. Movable loot, such as livestock and humans, formed the main spoils of warfare. Cattle and slaves, along with craft goods and jewellery, were the trappings by which a high-born warrior displayed his wealth and status to his rivals and dependants. As far as living conditions were concerned, the Pictish nobles lived with their kinsfolk and retainers in dwellings protected by topography and artificial defences. Such sites were often the residences of kings, ruling petty kingdoms. The nobility were members of the leader's prominent families in a particular area and some of them fought their way to power and called themselves monarchs. Lavish feasts were important rituals taking place in the presence of dignitaries.

The Pictish kings were not supported by any kind of bureaucracy, and had no civil service to administer their lands; trusted family friends advised the king when required, but he was essentially a lone figure who ruled in accordance with his personality. Any sign of weakness in battle meant that a king or warrior could be replaced with a more vigorous rival; the great kings of the Early Historic Period were ruthless leaders who conquered lands in the face of the enemy. Pictish success in warfare brought a constant flow of booty back to Pictland, making their henchmen rich. One historian of modern times suggested that the normal expectation of the seventh-century king was to die in battle. This observation was made in reference to Northumbria – the only Anglo-Saxon region to share a border with Pictland.

The nature of kingship was itself dramatic rather than static; it evolved and changed as the larger kingdoms of Britain and Ireland moved along the road to proto-statehood, but in the sixth century this process was in its infancy, and some kingdoms had only been formed as a result of the Roman withdrawal. From the sixth century onwards in continental Europe, and from the sixth century in southern Britain, kingship accelerated as a result of the spread of Christianity. Conversion to the Church within the Roman Empire became a major factor in the development of new ways for barbarian kings to rule their kingdoms. However, the Picts were slow to embrace the faith, and clung to paganism for a longer time than their neighbours. During the sixth century the trail of history resumes at a point where Pictish kings begin to emerge as real figures whose names and deeds appear in the sources.

During the period of the earliest kings, historians usually regard these men as over-kings, whose authority was acknowledged not only in their own kingdoms, but also in the lands of subordinate kings. This phenomenon may have seen the Picts as forming a power over a wide area. But sovereignty could be divided between two rivals. Pictland may have been a little smaller. Some Pictish over-kings might have ruled little more than one small region, such as Atholl or Fortriu.

The list of kings starts in the mythological period with a ruler called Gud and ends with an historical king called Drust in the mid ninth century. Drust's reign coincided with the rise to power of Cinead mac Alpin, a controversial figure who ruled Pictland and the Scots simultaneously. Gud stands at the head of the list, but is unknown in other sources. Gud was invented by the list's writers when the Picts extended their sequence of names backwards to give Pictish over-kings a more ancient origin. Each king in the list is given a reign length in years. Some kings appear in some sources, but not in others. Only when the name of a king can be linked securely to a definite historical date is the king's reign considered factual. The Irish Annals, for instance, associate many Pictish kings with real and dateable events; Gud is not recorded in the historical list, so the earlier kings are regarded as mythological. The annals list the death of Brude in Columba's time in the sixth century, the date 584 being recorded. He is recorded as having a reign of thirty years, which would place his accession in the mid 550s.

If the first twenty or so obscure kings are ignored as fictional, the list eventually records the name of Wradech, who appears in the Irish Annals too. The Pictish kings may be more than a myth in the prehistoric period for they appear to be active before the fifth century. Nothing more can be said of Wradech, but of the two kings who follow him in the list no other sources speak. If these two kings existed, their reigns may have been in the first half of the fifth century; one is Gartnait and the other is Talorc – two names which become common in later parts of the list. In the historical period, mention is made of the bishop Patrick, who had arrived in Ireland, and the Picts may have had more knowledge of him. The arrival of Patrick in Ireland may be put at between 431 and 470; he may have completed his mission by the time a king called Drust ruled the Picts.

To King Drust the list attributes 100 battles and an unlikely reign of 100 years. With him the list draws to a close at the end of the fifth century – a period when Christianity was firmly established in northern Britain.

Two texts attributed to St Patrick – his *Confession* and his letter to a British chieftain – have survived; these provide an insight into the work of a missionary in Ireland among 'barbarians'. By birth Patrick was a Briton of wealthy parentage, from a landowning family. History records that Patrick was captured as a slave by Irish raiders in the late fourth century, and was enslaved at Slemish in Ireland. He escaped to France, only to return again to the island as a missionary, as a bishop of the Catholic Church, sent to Erin by Pope Celestine I. He spent about thirty years evangelizing the Gaelic pagans, where he set up his Gaelic Church.

Patrick was acquainted with the Picts, but held them in a dim light. The Picts appear to have been active raiders. Medieval tradition refers to Patrick's disciple St Kessog as having undertaken missionary work in northern Britain, but this may not have extended to the Picts. Kessog is said to have founded a church in the territory of the Britons on the western shores of Loch Lomond – a tradition that can be supported by the finding of gravestones in the churchyard. In Pictland Kessog is associated with the church at Auchterarder and with the medieval fair at Callander, but there is no proof that he travelled as far eastwards. It is likely that his mission extended only to Luss and its environs, all of which lay in the territory of the Britons. It appears that neither they nor any of St Patrick's alleged disciples had tried to convert the Picts, but, as we shall see, other missionaries may have been less reluctant. The list of Pictish kings shows that Drust, son of Erp, was succeeded by another Talorc, to be followed by Morbet, also a son of Erp, but there was little love lost between these two men. In one of the texts Drust banished Nechtan from Pictland for reasons that were not apparent. The banishment appears to have served a useful purpose in bringing Nechtan to the monastery of Kildare in Ireland. Here this exiled prince is said to have met St Bridget of Kildare, one of the most famous figures in Gaelic Christianity in Erin; she foretold that he would one day rule the Picts in a time of peace.

St Bridget is a figure of the sixth and seventh centuries, Nechtan also being active at this time. Nechtan eventually went home to claim the kingship, and during the first years of his reign he saw the arrival in Pictland of a Christian mission from Kildare. The Gaelic missionaries from Ireland were led by an abbess called Darlugdach, one of Bridget's disciples, who received from Nechtan a grant of land where she could set up a church; from this base the Christians proceeded to evangelize the Picts. Her church was built at Abernethy, where in years to come a monastery flourished under the patronage of Pictish kings. Today there is a prominent round tower here dating to the eleventh century – an impressive sandstone structure which looms above the present-day

Kirk of St Bridget (Bride). Darlugdach's foundation would have been a typical outpost of the ancient Gaelic Church – a simple wooden building enclosed by a fence or earthwork.

To cloud these facts, different traditions give various accounts of the foundation of early churches and monasteries. Abernethy's kirk carries a dedication to St Bridget and is one of the many Scottish churches whose traditions date back to Bridget of Kildare. The place name Kilbride derives from her missionary work among the Picts. During the ninth and tenth centuries the Vikings attacked the Picts, making settlements also elsewhere in Scotland. Bridget was much venerated by Christians of Hiberno-Norse extraction; many churches bear her name in the form of Bride. From the ninth century onwards the Picts increasingly adopted the Gaelic language and culture of their neighbours – the Scots of Argyll – and may have taken an interest in other Irish saints. The ruined medieval church at Blair Atholl is known as St Bride's Kirk and occupies an inland site in the heart of Pictland, but the dedication to Bridget is not recorded before 1275. Likewise, Kilbride in Strathearn lies within a southern Pictish province or subkingdom. Another factor to be kept in mind is that there were more than a dozen Gaelic saints called Bridget in addition to the Abbess of Kildare.

Nechtan Morbet also makes an appearance in the ecclesiastical history, but is of questionable origin. We can gain information about Pictland from the *Vita*, or life, of St Boethius, an Irishman that hailed from a royal kingdom in Munster in south-west Ireland, but it is not a biography in the modern sense. These sources must be treated with caution, for they are works of hagiography rather than straight history. These sources appear to advertize the life of holy men, rather than accounts of secular life. The account of Boethius's life is typical of this. It was composed several centuries after the saint's passing, and it survives in manuscript form to the present day. Boethius is a little-known saint who, according to the annals, died in 521, the year when AD dating came into existence. In his *Vita* he is said to have brought back to life a ruler called Nectanus, who might be Nechtan Morbet of the list of kings; Boethius established a church in a place assumed to be Kirkbuddo, a Roman fort south-east of Forfar, whose name derives from a term meaning Fort of Boethius, near the ancient stronghold of Dunnichen Hill. Again, information about this is questionable for it was compiled by writers who were not historians.

Another early saint with a Pictish connection was Fillan, a monk from Ireland who lived in either the fifth or sixth century. In Pictland he is associated with the fort of Dundurn in a village in Strathearn; excavations have provided us with some information about the period. This hill fort occupies a site near a ruined church known as St Fillan's Chapel, of great antiquity, whose origins are unknown, but it is possible that it played a role in Fillan's work when he undertook the evangelization of the Picts of Strathearn. The various references to missionary campaigns led by Darlugdach, Boethius and Fillan suggest that these saints were the first to bring Christianity to the Picts, but again sources may be spurious. On the other hand most hagiography contains traces of the myths and inventions of earlier years.

The Venerable Bede believed that the southern Picts were Christianized by a Briton called Ninian, but the northern Picts were not evangelized until the mission of St Columba in about 565. Columba came from the monastic school of Iona in the Scottish islands. Bede is quite a reliable source. However, he may have been unaware of the events in Pictland before the time of

Ninian and Columba. Bede records that the mission of Ninian was the first successful mission to Pictland. Bede believed that the nation was divided into two parts by the Grampian Mountains. This imposing mountain range forms a natural division between Perthshire and the northeast Highlands; how far the barrier served as a political or cultural boundary across Pictland is hard to assess, but Bede clearly regarded it as a dividing line. For him there was a dividing line between those converted by Ninian and those converted by Columba. Ninian is a controversial figure who continues to provoke debate among historians. Bede says that he was a Briton who was buried with other saints at Candida Casa (The White House), a place now at Whithorn in Galloway, and it was here that a monastery flourished at Ninian's shrine or tomb.

Also in the eighth century, a monk of Candida Casa composed a Latin poem – 'The Miracle of Bishop Ninian' – which identified the saint's Pictish converts as members of a people called the Naturae. Later still, when Galloway became part of the medieval kingdom of Scotland, the shrine of Whithorn attracted pilgrims inspired by accounts of the life of St Ninian. The Venerable Bede's statements about St Ninian's mission to the Picts can be reinforced by archaeological evidence of early Christianity in Galloway and in southern parts of Pictland. Excavations at Candida Casa reveal evidence of a monastery there until about 500. Other accounts about missions to the Picts are not as reliable as Bede's. Like all hagiographies, their main concern was to enhance the character of the writers' favourite saints and their achievements.

The lives of Ninian and Kentigern (a later saint) incorporate miracle stories and monkish folklore, and therefore serve their genre well. Pilgrims to Candida Casa brought home souvenirs, and the cult of relics was perhaps strong. They may not have been as unbelieving about whether Ninian converted the Picts in the fifth century. They would not have questioned the traditions reported by Bede and others, such as Ailred and Jocelin. An examination of the sources suggests that there was folklore which may or may not have been derived from real events. In the case of Ninian it is conjectured that Galloway was also the home of the Picts. It places Ninian in the vicinity of the saint's tomb at Candida Casa. In actual fact the people of Galloway were Britons whose ancestors were recorded in Ptolemy's map under the name of Novantae.

After the withdrawal of the Roman Empire, these tribes regarded the Picts with hostility, as pirates and brigands who plundered their coastlands. For some time, perhaps, after the twelfth century, English people regarded the Picts as inhabitants of Galloway. Medieval England had little knowledge of the political situation in Scotland with regard to the Picts. As a contemporary of the Candida Casa English monks, Bede knew that the monastery lay among the Britons, the descendants of the Novantae, so he was sure of the Galloway Picts, with regard to their existence. But from where did he derive his information about the Picts and the mission of Ninian? One source may have been Pecthelm, an Englishman and a contemporary of Bede, who served as Bishop of Candida Casa, or Whithorn, in the eighth century. Other sources were Pictish priests that were communicating with Bede's own monastery at Jarrow, but the chronology of the mission is missing.

Bede was writing in his *Ecclesiastical History of the English People*, and recorded the mission to Pictland; all he could say was that Ninian worked among the Picts for a number of years before the arrival of St Columba about 565. Ninian thus has gone into history as a missionary from Britain who converted part of the Pictish nation in the early 500s, before retiring to his monastery at Candida Casa in Galloway. Ninian was of noble birth, preaching to the upper classes of Pictland. After some time he received permission from the Pictish ruling classes to convert the common people. A grant of land would enable Ninian to set up churches and monasteries in the countryside. But now the conversion had been halted, and Ninian had retired to his monastery in Galloway. Archaeological evidence may uncover some sixth-century activity of later missions, but this information may linger in the uncertain realm of legend.

In the list of Pictish kings there is a second king called Drust, whose reign may have extended into the early sixth century, but there is not much known about him, nor about his successors. The next two kings also bear the name Drust, and are said to have held the kingship jointly, presumably ruling parts of Pictland at the same time; they are figures of the early sixth century.

A certain King Drust figures in an Irish tale about Finnian of Moville. The setting of this tale is also in Whithorn in Galloway. Candida Casa Monastery is seen as operating under the authority of an Irish abbot called Mugint and with Irish monks such as Finnian among the brethren. The story revolves around a daughter of Drust: the princess was sent to Whithorn by her father to become a pupil of Mugint, but she fell in love with one of the monks. The tale originated in monastic folklore of unknown origin and probably only contains a small degree of actual history. Other Irish (Gaelic) sources tell how Finnian studied at Whithorn in his youth.

The King's daughter Drustric appears in another Irish text, where she is said to have become the mother of a Galloway saint called Lonan. Whether she existed is hard to determine, but the name Drust is Pictish rather than British; her father was perhaps meant to become one of the Drusts whom the list of kings cites as ruling Pictland in the early sixth century. The next six kings in the list are given very short reigns, and nothing is known of them. One of them ruled the Picts for three years before sharing his reign with Brude. He was the son of Maelchon.

Brude is the first Pictish king to enter the pages of authentic history, and more is known about him than the other rulers. The start of his reign in 554 marks the point where Pictish history finally emerges from the era of legend and uncertainty. The middle of the sixth century marks the period in which Pictish history becomes clearer; from c.550 information becomes more reliable, chiefly because some of the more important sources began to be written around this date. This was the age in which the Irish monasteries were producing a number of manuscripts about the history of Gaelic peoples. Bede, who was born in the seventh century, drew upon these sources. The later half of the sixth century appears as less of a mystery than the preceding era.

In 563 St Columba left his monastery at Derry to found his famous school on Iona in the Scottish islands. According to Bede he preached the faith to kingdoms of the northern Picts. Bede believed that the southern Picts had already been evangelized by St Ninian, as previously stated, which might explain the presence of early Christian cemeteries in Fife and Angus. With the coming of Columba in the sixth century, the Picts had been ruled for eight or nine years by Brude, son of Maelchon, whom Bede called a most powerful king. The list of Pictish kings and the Irish Annals give Brude a reign of three decades, putting his death at 584. Maelchon would have lived in the early sixth century, but does not appear in the list as a Pictish king. The name Maelchon is quite rare, and it may have Welsh origins.

The fate of these early kings was decided by a great plague that swept through the British Isles in 547, when they perished because of the pestilence. Maelchon enters history in the first half of the sixth century, and the Welsh king Maelcon may have the same origins as Maelchon. The circumstances that may have led to royal marriage between Wales and Pictland are not easy to explain. There is no known connection between Maelgwn and northern Britain, but this does not make his marriage to a Pictish monarch any less likely. It is likely that he spent some time among the Picts in his youth, perhaps as an exile seeking sanctuary, and thus came into contact with the painted people.

The only records of dealings between Wales and Pictland appear in the *Historia Brittonum*, a history of the Britons which was carefully written by a Welsh monk in c.830, based on earlier material. This work records that Irish raiders were expelled from Wales after having settled there. A number of small kingdoms were set up. These 'facts' have been discredited by modern historians as pieces of fiction created in the eighth century, concocted by the kings to establish their position in the countryside and to enhance the position of the royal family of Gwynedd.

Gwynedd was superior to the other Welsh kingdoms.

Post-Roman historians have traced links between Pictland and Wales. Inter-dynastic marriage was a regular feature of the Dark Ages or the Early Historic Period. It is no surprise that at least some Welsh kings were producing a crown prince for the Picts.

Let us turn to the Scots of Dalriada. At this time, the sixth century, in the reign of the Pictish King Brude, Columba visited Pictland at a time when there was war between the Picts and the Scots. Columba's monastery of Iona lay in the lands of the Scots, and relied on the support of the Scottish kings. In Brude's time there was not, of course, an entity known as Scotland, but there were in the far western parts of northern Britain people that called themselves Scots. They were enemies of High King Brude, which needs to be explained. It involves an examination of their society, their culture and their origins. Who were the Scots? The Scots in the west have been traditionally cited as Irish colonists. In Roman times the label 'Scotti' was applied by the Latin writers to speakers of Gaelic, denoting the inhabitants of Ireland. It has been asserted that the Gaelic speakers of Ireland gave their Gaelic-speaking peoples the language of western Scotland, chiefly its islands.

Gaelic still survives in the Gaidhealtachd areas of Scotland, mainly in the Western Isles, where it can be heard in everyday speech. But did it really arrive in Britain no earlier than the fifth century? According to the origin legend, a dynasty of Gaelic kings from Antrim in north-east Ireland set up a kingdom in Argyll probably in the fifth century AD, calling it Scottish Dalriada after the parent kingdom of Antrim Dalriada. This dynasty also established kingdoms in Cowal, Kintyre and Islay, grouped together as Scottish Dalriada, its Gaelic name deriving from the Dal Riata. The Scots were to emerge as the dominant power in Argyll, and in later centuries as masters of northern Britain.

The Venerable Bede includes a version of the origin legend in his ecclesiastical history of 731, in which he refers to an Irish tribe called Reuda acquiring land in Pictish areas either by negotiation or by the sword. These settlers took the leader's name and called themselves Dalreudini – a name peculiar to Bede. Sources attribute the founding of the Scottish colony to the Gaelic Fergus mac Erc, who has been identified as Dalriada's first king. A medieval genealogy of Fergus places him tenth in succession from a king called Coirpre Riata and thirteenth in succession after the founder of the Antrim kingdom. Under the year 501, the Gaelic or Irish Annals place Fergus as occupying some territory in Britain, and he died there. By the Columban age in the sixth century the Scottish Dalriada kings were well established. The Gaels now looked eastwards. The ambitious elite spoke Gaelic – the language of Ireland, or Erin – and bore Irish names. It was easy for Bede and others to believe that Fergus mac Erc originated from County Antrim. However, modern archaeology supports the idea that there was little activity between Argyll and north-east Ireland. There are few archaeological remains to support an Irish/Scottish Dalriada.

The types of settlement that are typical of Ireland during the sixth century are not found in Argyll. There is nothing to show that the area underwent a great change of population during the first millennium AD; nor is there any evidence for a seizure of power in Argyll by a small but vigorous power from Ireland. For example, archaeology shows that in the Dark Ages or Early Historic Period among the Gaels of Ireland the aristocracy fastened their cloaks with a peculiar type of brooch, which differed from types worn in Britain. In Argyll it is the British design, not the Irish, that comes to light.

Archaeology cannot support a colonization process in Scottish Dalriada. Nor do linguists see any sign of language change, which occurs when one culture colonizes another. The theorists believe that Scottish Dalriada was not a significant power in the west of Scotland and that place names would have been cited by the ancient historians. Perhaps these early peoples were not of Irish origin, but it has been the belief of most historians that Argyll was colonized from Antrim or Irish Dalriada. The view can be held that this region of Argyll was already populated by Gaelic-speaking Scots before the fifth century, when Fergus mac Erc is said to have set up Scottish Dalriada.

If the modern view is correct, what is the relationship between them and the Picts? For the answer to this question one must cast a glance back to Roman times and Ptolemy's map of Scotland. The map shows that the region was inhabited by the Epidii. It seems to be true that the Epidii were ousted by an influx of Gaelic-speaking colonists from Antrim three or four centuries later. The Epidii may have spoken Gaelic in Roman times and simply re-emerged in the later historic period of the Dark Ages of Scottish Dalriada. The latest view is that there was a Gaelic-speaking tribe in Argyll since prehistoric times, consistent with the geography of north-west Britain.

For the people of Argyll it must have been hard to establish relations with Pictland, but the coast of County Antrim lies only thirteen miles from the Mull of Kintyre, which is clearly visible from the Irish mainland. Long before Roman times north-east Ireland was the nearest neighbour to the people of Argyll. In early times the North Channel was a uniting line between the folk of north-east Ireland and the west of Scotland. Trade and interaction gave these communities dependence on the seaways that did not act as a barrier, so it is not hard to realize how Gaelic became the common language of Argyll. If the inhabitants of Argyll were already Gaelic-speaking before the fifth century there may not have been an influx of settlers from Ireland. Historians now take the view that the Fergus mac Erc colonization originated in the 730s rather than the fifth or sixth century. Bede's eighth-century version of the legend – the earliest known – was perhaps created by the Scots of his own time to justify territorial claims on Irish Dalriada. The legend sees their kingdom in Argyll as an offshoot of the motherland in County Antrim.

It has been claimed that Dalriada in Ireland was a colony of its namesake in Britain rather than vice versa. It appears that the Picts and Scots of Argyll had indigenous roots in Scotland in their respective lands, but their cultures travelled along separate lines. The harsh geography of the Scottish Highlands kept these two peoples apart, and they did not speak the same language. The Picts spoke a language akin to that of the Britons beyond their southern borders, and the two dialects were to some extent mutually intelligible. The forms of their settlements and the designs of their jewellery gave them an affinity with people elsewhere in coastal areas of Britain, but their speech made them appear Irish. Throughout the Roman period they had some kind of relationship with the Picts, and perhaps engaged in small-scale trade across Drium Alban.

But now the Dalriada kings looked east in the sixth century to threaten their existence. Before AD 500 the Scots were merely one of many Gaelic-speaking communities along the northern shores of the Irish Sea, mainly located in Britain rather than in Ireland. Their main trade was with the little communities, and they engaged in seaborne raids; each of these little kingdoms had its own royal dynasty. These kindred were known as Cenela, meaning 'tribal area'. In the sixth century there was much competition between the kingdoms for the kingship of Dalriada. There was much economic pressure on the land. It was not long before the arrogant men of Dalriada waged war against the Picts. The Irish Annals tell a tale of warfare around the year 559.

Little is known about the heirs of Fergus mac Erc, but one Gabran was regarded by the annalists as being of sufficient importance for his death to be recorded; the annals of 559 are of significance because they contain the earliest report of a clash of arms between the Picts and the Scots, but its location is not given. The outcome is clear, for Brude had won and the Scots retreated. It is perhaps true that the battle of 559 marked a decisive Pictish victory over Dalriada to acknowledge Brude as High King.

It was during Brude's reign that St Columba brought the Church to the northern Picts. He was a Gael of noble birth. If he had not chosen a religious career he would have continued to be a warrior, perhaps even a king. He was born in 521, and began training for the priesthood while still young. He had a fierce ambition, but he was humble. He left his homeland in 563 for unknown reasons and sailed to Scotland with a small band of religious folk. He set up what was to become the famous monastery and school of Iona. Most of what we know about his life comes from the work of St Adomnán, a seventh-century Abbot of Iona, but he is also mentioned by the Venerable Bede in the seventh century. It is through his *Vita Columbae* that modern historians obtain most of their information about Columba or Columcille. The Iona monastery was situated in west Argyll, off the coast of Mull. According to the Irish Annals the Iona foundation was a gift from Conall, son of Comgall, the over-king of Dalriada; Bede says that it was a gift from Brude, but this is perhaps a later version created by the Picts to portray Iona as part of their territory.

Iona is well removed from Pictland, but Columba was a Gaelic-speaker along with the Picts. By establishing his Iona monastery Columba was not so much seeking a springboard for missionary work among the Picts as aligning himself with the powerful elites of Dalriada. His closest bonds were with the tribes of the Mull of Kintyre; for some years Kintyre was the premier royal house of this dynasty. Bede places Columba's mission to the Picts in 565, two years after his arrival in Scotland. The conversions were not a single event at which the entire Pictland was evangelized, but rather a long process of travelling and preaching.

Columba convinced High King Brude to abandon his pagan ways and to forsake the Shamanists (a lower form of Druidism). Columba made the sign of the cross before the gates of Brude's palace and the gates flew open, but in hagiography terms this was a small miracle. Adomnán states that Brude was much impressed with Columba and Christianity, so he welcomed the pilgrims into his realm. It is likely that Brude had prior knowledge of the mission from Iona, and that he prepared to welcome the Gaelic saint and his Gaelic Church. Both Brude and Columba were royals. They carried out high-status relationships common to the sixth century in the Early Historic Period or the Dark Ages.

The old gods of Pictland were perhaps in decline in Scotland when Columba presented his credentials. In every corner of the British Isles paganism was retreating in the face of the Church; Brude may have realized that Christianity was making inroads, especially after the fall of West Rome in the early years of the fifth century. But Brude may have regarded Christ as one of his many gods, the Church having a very special relationship with the High Kingship of Pictland.

Adomnán sees the conflict between Columba and the Shamanists as a face-to-face conflict between paganism and the Church of Rome, with its pagan roots. The chief Shamanist was Broichan, Brude's own foster-father, who continued to resent Columba even after Columba managed to save him miraculously from death. Brude gave Columba permission to evangelize his empire, and many folk in his palace were baptized by the saint. Brude may have remained mainly a pagan until his death – perhaps a matter of personal choice to earn the goodwill of some of the Pictish elite who did not want change. Bede describes Brude as a powerful king, for he received homage from a number of subsidiary Pictish kings. He had a ferocious ambition and ruled with an iron touch.

Over-kingship of this period was not hereditary, but had to be earned by success in battle. Some feuds were internal ones and every king had to contend with them where they rose up inside Pictland. A king that waged successful war was likely to become an overlord in a wide domain. This was how Brude achieved his position as High King of Pictland. Other feuds took place as enemies tried to invade Pictland from further afield. In warfare a king of the Dark Ages commanded by force and reputation. There were no governmental structures as in modern times. Adomnán speaks of a Pictish council accompanying Brude during Columba's mission, but these men were senior warriors rather than bureaucrats or administrators. Brude's achievement perhaps fell apart after his death.

The extent of his authority can be gleaned from the *Vita*

Columbae in a story told about one Cormac and some other Ionian monks. Columba told Brude that Cormac and some other Ionian monks wanted to sail away to remote places to establish monasteries and churches. Among those present at Brude's court was the under-king of Orkney, the Regulus, into whose territories Cormac wanted to go. This king was in communication with the Pictish over-king. Neither Adomnán nor others record Brude as warring in Orkney, but sometime during his reign he subjected the islands to his rule.

There is little doubt that the inhabitants of Orkney, or the Orcadians, regarded themselves as Pictish; at the Brough of Birsay, a high-status site on the largest island in the group, there is a carved stone with four Pictish symbols and representations of three spear-bearing warriors that once stood in the old graveyard. The carvings date from the seventh and eighth centuries, and they are thus later than Brude's reign. It is thought that Orcadia was an important residence of Orcadian kings. Columba visited Brude at one of his fortresses near the mouth of the River Ness, but it is not named in the *Vita*; it may have been a hill fort. Some historians think that it was situated near Inverness. Excavations reveal that there were remains dating to this period in the fourth century AD. Despite the discovery of a metalworking mound, the site seems to have been abandoned in the 500s. It has cast doubt on the theory that this was where Brude met Columba. A site at Craig Phadrig for the meeting does not seem to be very convincing, and there are also two other likely places, one of these being Castle Hill near Inverness. The other is the hill fort of Torvean.

The image of Brude holding court beside the River

Ness has led to the belief that his domain lay in northern Pictland. However, neither Brude nor Adomnán states that he held court south of the Mounth. The royal courts were itinerant, which enabled the kings to keep their subjects and lords in check. Brude's fortress on the River Ness seems to be one of these sites. Southern Pictland seems to have been an important power base – an area of good agricultural land, and thus a key source of revenue for Pictish kings. The area of Fortriu, identified with Moray, may be assumed to have been Brude's home territory. The name Brude was borne by a number of Pictish kings and may have been especially associated with this area, and perhaps Brude himself hailed from Fortriu and was a northern Pict by birth. If so, his fortress near the River Ness was probably an ancestral residence well situated for dealing with sub-kings from Orkney and other northerly districts. How far Brude's Pictland extended westwards is not known.

During his reign there was warfare between Pictland and Scottish Dalriada and pressure from the Scots in frontier areas; these regions may have included the Isle of Skye, which was most likely peopled by Picts at this time. Three stones bearing Pictish symbols have been uncovered, and there is additional information from Adomnán in his story of Columba meeting one Artbranan, who arrived in Skye in a small boat when the saint was visiting the island. But after being baptized he died and was buried on the spot. It is probable that he spoke a language other than Gaelic, for there is a record of interpreters. He was an aristocratic leader of a war band, and he may have been answerable to Brude.

There is a possibility that Artbranan had already

acknowledged the King of Cenel nGabrain as his new overlord and he felt compelled to show this allegiance by seeking baptism from their spiritual patriarch. However, there is little information about Brude's 'empire'. In the *Vita Columbae* some pagans were encountered by Columba on the banks near Loch Ness. Here the saint performed further baptisms; these people were retainers and tenant farmers and other dependants; the family's home may have been at the ruins of Urquhart at the mouth of the glen.

Adomnán's brief allusions do not give any indication of the success of the Columban mission, despite the establishment of a number of monasteries and churches in Pictland. The monastery of Deer in Buchan claimed Columba as its founding father and supported this claim by a suitable legend. Deer was certainly an important foundation in later Pictish times, and sometime around AD 900 its monks produced an illuminated manuscript of the Gospels, known today as the *Book of Deer*.

Columba was assisted in his mission by a Pict called St Drostan. There is little known about this saint, and historians cannot confirm that he existed outside folklore, although the notes in the *Book of Deer* perhaps preserve local traditions of much older origin. The foundation story claims Drostan as a disciple of Columba on his travels in Pictland. On the coast of Buchan the local lord provided these two saints with a grant of land to establish a foundation. A second monastery was also founded at Deer, twelve miles to the south. Other traditions identify Drostan as a Scot of royal blood who had been educated in Ireland, although his name suggests Pictish ancestry, but he spent his final years as a hermit at Glenesk in Angus.

The Deer story may be based on true events in the sixth century embellished by layers of theological folklore. A Pictish monastery once stood there, perhaps founded by St Columba during the reign of High King Brude. The mysterious Drostan may have accompanied him to assist in missionary work and to act as an interpreter.

Many of Iona's monks were newly baptized Christians; others bore Pictish names. Many sites in the Highlands are connected with Columba's name; his Gaelic name was Columb Cille, 'Dove of the Church'. Bede and others cite Columba as the founder of a number of churches along with later Pictish monasteries founded in the eighth century – mostly daughter houses of the Iona monastery. A Gaelic poem called the *'Amrae Columb Cille'*, 'The Praise of Columba', was composed within a few years of his death in 597, and credits him with converting the tribes of the Tay region, but there are not many archaeological remains.

It seems likely that foundations, if they existed, were the works of later evangelists sent from Iona in the seventh century. Another explanation may be that Columba laboured primarily north of Mounth, in the same region where Brude maintained a rural residence on the River Ness, of which Deer was perhaps one. The Pictish kings of later centuries adopted Columba as their mentor for his missionary activities in the Highlands; within 100 years of his death the cult of Columba was well established in Britain and Ireland. Revered as a great saint, he was to eventually become the patron saint of Scotland.

Let us turn to political events in Pictland. In 574, King Conaill of Dalriada had died and was succeeded by his cousin Aedan mac Grabrain, a member of the Kintyre dynasty. Columba ordained Aedan as King of Cenel nGabrain in a ceremony on Iona. Aedan had great ambitions for he soon launched attacks upon his neighbours, at length challenging the authority of the High King of the Picts, the converted Brude. In 580 he attacked the Orkneys, which were under Brude's rule. The High King of the Picts died in 584, perhaps in battle rather than peacefully. His successor was Garnait, who repulsed an attack on Pictland in 598. Within a few years Garnait too was dead, and his passing is noted in the annals at AD 600, coinciding with the Battle of Degastan, where Aedan was decisively defeated by the northern English. Bede writes that the battle was a great turning point in Scottish history.

In the early seventh century the English shared no common frontier with the Picts; the two kingdoms were separated by Gododdin, the largest British kingdom, whose territory included Lothian and the great citadel of Din Eidyn on the site now occupied by Edinburgh Castle. But the English had minor victories in the closing years of the sixth century. Historians usually identify Catraeth, the site of a battle, as Catterick, in Yorkshire. A poem was composed about the event, and survives today as an account of one of the most controversial battles in Scottish history in the Early Historic Period. Several additions to the poem were made along with alterations. The poem is more commonly known as 'The Gododdin'. This has not deterred some historians from treating the poem as the authentic diary of a sixth-century war correspondent, but this is not likely.

One verse in 'The Gododdin' refers to a man named

Budon, who may have been a Pict fighting alongside the Britons at the Battle of Catraeth. He is described by the poet as hailing from beyond the Sea of Iddew. Budon appears to be a Pictish ally of the Britons, perhaps a free-booting nobleman after wealth and reputation. The poem, however, sheds no light on the relations between Pictland and Gododdin at the time of the battle. At all times there would have been hostilities between the two kingdoms in what is now Stirlingshire, alternating with periods of uneasy peace. By AD 600 the Britons of Lothian were steadily giving ground to the Kingdom of Bernica; their defeat at Catraeth was only one episode that was to culminate in the final collapse of Gododdin. Now the Picts would come face-to-face with a more aggressive people – but that is another story to be told in a future book.

SELECT BIBLIOGRAPHY

A. MacDonald, *Curadán, Boniface and the Early Church of Rosemarkie* (Rosemarkie, 1992).

A. Macquarrie, *The Saints of Scotland, AD 450–1093* (Edinburgh, 1997).

A. Woolf, *The Churches of Pictavia* (Cambridge, 2013).

B. E. Crawford (editor), *Conversion and Christianity in the North Sea World* (St Andrews, 1998).

I. Finlay, *Columba* (London, 1979).

K. Hughes, *Early Christianity in Pictland* (Jarrow, 1970).

M. Carver, *Portmahomack: Monastery of the Picts* (Edinburgh, 2008).

R. Sharpe (editor), *Life of St Columba* by Adomnán of Iona (London, 1995).

T. Clarkson, *Columba* (Edinburgh, 2012).

NOTES

NOTES

NOTES

NOTES

NOTES

NOTES

NOTES